D1827157

What are people saying about Faith—A Lion's Healing Journey Back To Innocence

With Faith, all things are possible.

Who knew the story of a lioness could teach so much?

Faith's healing journey made me cry first with sadness and then with jubilation.

Through reading this simple story, I learned to accept that neither myself or anyone else will ever be perfect.

I finally get the "forgiveness thing" after years of anger.

Faith taught me victimization is a choice.

I learned there are worse fates than being alone, such as: remaining in an abusive relationship.

Knowing why abusers abuse has helped me to forgive my ex-husband.

I was molested as a child, but after reading Faith—A Lion's Healing Journey Back To Innocence, I am finally free of guilt and shame.

I took Goldstein's advise . . . I gave my "damaged inner child up for adoption."

Without Faith, I'd still be unhappy and self-destructive.

Faith really works . . . I highly recommend this book. And the artwork is amazing.

Faith taught me to stop judging myself and others from a standard, which used to set me up for disappointment.

Forgiving and remembering was the key to breaking my pattern of being in unhealthy relationships.

If Faith can forgive her abuser, so can I.

Now that I've reclaimed my innocence through reading Faith—A Lion's Healing Journey, I see others as innocent as well.

My abusive step-father died over twenty years ago and finally I was able to forgive him his trespasses.

Reading Faith's journey allowed me to forgive my alcoholic mother. While fighting her own issues, under the circumstances, she did the best she could.

I thought Goldstein's Male Thing Explained was great, but Faith—A Lion's Healing Journey helped me even more to overcome my demons.

If you wish to find joy in your life, have Faith on your bookshelf and periodically re-read it for renewed strength.

I've finally let my "healthy inner child come out to play." It's fun to laugh again like when I was a kid.

Faith—A Lion's Healing Journey Back To Innocence taught me why I was a bully as a child and why I abused my first wife as an adult.

I now understand childhood traumas don't have the power to hurt me . . . only my attitude about what happened in the past can sabotage my happiness.

I could relate to Faith's dilemma; the decision to change can be daunting, but well worth the effort.

Faith demonstrated that with an attitude of forgiveness, time can mend a broken heart and heal a damaged spirit.

For Ruth — a creative spirit
with a loving heart.

Edward Lee Goldstein

Faith–A Lion's Healing Journey
Back To Innocence

Lessons On Forgiveness

814. 749.5653

EdwardLeeGee@Aim.Com

Faith–A Lion's Healing Journey Back To Innocence

Lessons On Forgiveness

Edward Lee Goldstein, MA, MS, RPT.

First Edition

LITAS-HART Publishing
Sherman Oaks, California

Faith–A Lion's Healing Journey Back To Innocence

Lessons On Forgiveness

Edward Lee Goldstein, MA, MS, RPT.

Published by:

LITAS-HART PUBLISHING
PO Box 55066
Sherman Oaks, California 91413   USA.
Website: **FaithandForgivenessThingExplained.com**
Email: **AskEdward@FaithandForgivenessThingExplained.com**
Phone toll free: **(888) 222-4001**

All rights reserved. No part of this book may be duplicated or utilized in any form or by any means, electronic or mechanical, including photocopying, recording, or by any information storage and retrieval system, without written permission from the author, except for the inclusion of brief quotations in a review.

Copyright © Edward Lee Goldstein, 2013
Cover Illustration copyright © Edward Lee Goldstein, 2013
Cover Design copyright © Edward Lee Goldstein, 2013
Book Illustrations copyright © Edward Lee Goldstein, 2013
First Printing 2013
Printed in the United States of America

Publisher's Cataloging-in-Publication
(Provided by Quality Books, Inc.)

    Goldstein, Edward Lee.
      Faith, a lion's healing journey back to innocence :
   lessons on forgiveness / Edward Lee Goldstein. -- 1st ed.

     p. cm.
     Includes bibliographical references.
     ISBN-13: 978-0-9712315-7-3
     ISBN-10: 0-9712315-7-5

     1. Forgiveness. 2. Interpersonal relations.
    3. Faith. I. Title.

   BF637.F67G65 2013   158.1
         QBI12-600074

Author's Message

I would like to thank you for allowing me to share *Faith — A Lion's Healing Journey Back To Innocence: Lessons On Forgiveness*. I have found we can only truly forgive what we fully understand. The healing process involves the workings of both our right, "intuitive," emotional brain, as well as our left, "logical," problem solving brain. For that reason, *Faith* is separated into two parts. Part One is *Faith's Journey,* an emotionally-charged metaphorical story about a young lioness—the right brain component. From the perspective of Faith, our lioness heroine, Part Two, *Our Journey With Faith* both explains and takes the reader through the left brain's intellectual mechanism of forgiving. By integrating both our emotions and logic, it is possible to effectively apply the lessons in this book to our own lives. As a Health Educator and "forgiveness expert," I have used this material both personally and professionally. Trust me, if one is receptive and desires greater joy and happiness, it is possible. As a by-product of forgiveness, emotional and physical healings have occurred; people's lives have been turned around.

My lifelong spiritual quest has been one of discovering ways to best utilize my knowledge, talents, and the healing gifts with which I've been blessed. I believe the purpose of the brotherhood of men and sisterhood of women is for us to teach and learn from each other about the joys of "humanhood," the meaning of Love.

My first book, *The Male Thing Explained* has helped many women and men with guilt, shame, anger, and relationship issues. Currently, with the publishing of *Faith—A Lion's Healing Journey Back To Innocence,* I'll soon be completing my third book, which addresses the questions my clients and audience most often ask about human behavior and why we do the things we do. The material in this new work-in-progress, *The Human Thing Explained: Taming the Lizard and the Dog, Forgiving and Living with Love* has already been tested and has been shown to be invaluable in raising consciousness and uplifting people's lives.

I greatly appreciate your emails to my website in the form of questions, comments, and shared wisdom. They play a vital role in this new project's evolution.

For inquiries regarding public or corporate speaking engagements, or working privately with Edward Lee Goldstein on relationship and forgiveness issues, physical therapy or other health related areas, visit his website:

Website: **FaithandForgivenessThingExplained.com**
Email: **AskEdward@FaithandForgivenessThingExplained.com**
Phone toll free: **(888) 222-4001**

I wish you joy, health, success, and hope for bright tomorrows.

Edward Lee Goldstein MA, MS, RPT

Dedication

This book is dedicated to the memory of my parents, Esther and Lewis, my grandmother, Ida, my wife, Mildred; my dearest friends, Carroll and Carmelita Haeske; and a sweet spirit and lover of animals great and small, Lois Constantine. It is further dedicated to all who have suffered at the hands of others or inadvertently from their own misguided choices. We are all products of our upbringing, environment . . . and, perhaps, fate. In embracing the truth we are "less than perfect" human beings, bound to make mistakes, I honor those who seek the tools needed to forgive others their trespasses. I respect those who own their mistakes, make amends when possible and appropriate, and desire to forgive themselves as part of the healing process. I applaud those who wish to learn the lessons inherent in their challenging experiences. I revere those who desire to improve the lot of others through sharing their stories and knowledge. I am in awe of those who recognize and live these three truths: To ere is human and to forgive divine; when we forgive our enemies quickly, we have no enemies. And finally, when we forgive ourselves, we become our own best friend. In essence, this book is dedicated to the resiliency of the human spirit and the transformative power of love.

Table of Contents

Acknowledgments

I begin with an appreciative round of applause, saluting the multitudes of Librarians who have shown me endless patience. Many thanks to my supportive audience, which has reported their many positive results from reading *The Male Thing Explained*—those kind souls who have encouraged me to continue sharing tangible information that improves lives. For their input, editing, and support I thank Cleo Baldon, my sister Sheila Friedman, Carol Soucek King, and Peggy Zuckerman, I acknowledge Irwin Zucker, "Book Publicist *extraordinaire*," and the founder of the Book Publicists of Southern California. I wish to express my praise and gratitude to Phil Wagner, Donald Maloney, Nathan Thibert, Karen Doyle and the rest of the Bang Printing family for their assistance and expertise associated with the printing of this book. A note of thanks goes out to Beverly Houwing, an Adobe Tech girl with a big heart. A special vote of appreciation goes to Dirk Baldon who has taught me more about patience than almost anyone I know. In personifying the benefits of hard work, dedication and focus, I acknowledge my brother and sister-in-law, Donald and Roberta Goldstein. As always, beyond words, I am forever cognizant of that Higher Power: Love, God, Truth, Spirit, Light—the Great I Am, which has provided me with this enigmatic Life Force—the One who has written this script through me, who has peopled my world with the cast of characters: women and men, mentors and nemeses. I honor the One who has allowed the information in this book to come alive . . . to heal all those who are destined to be receptive to its promise.

Warning—Disclaimer

Regarding *Faith—A Lion's Healing Journey Back to Innocence*, the author's intent is to entertain and educate. This book is being sold with the understanding that the writer and publisher are not providing any medical, psychological, spiritual, legal, or any other kind of counseling. If physical, mental, psychological, legal, or any other expert opinions are needed by the reader, it is strongly suggested he or she seek professional advice from experts in these fields.

Faith—A Lion's Healing Journey Back to Innocence is a fictional story and includes information, which the author found useful in his own life. This book should not be considered by the reader to be a "handbook on how to live *my* life." The author can assume no responsibility for anyone's health or happiness, but his own. Therefore the author and Litas-Hart Publishing shall not assume any liability to any individual or group, concerning any damage or alleged damage to have been caused directly or indirectly by the information contained in this book.

If you are not able to accept the above-mentioned constraints and recommendations, you should return this book to your point of purchase.

Part I
Faith's Journey

Not so long ago in a not so distant land, a primeval drama was unfolding—unfolding deep within the heart of the lush South African jungle. As a young lioness, Faith had been a popular, carefree little girl. With the passaging of the seasons, the turning of the leaves, now considered an adult, though surprised and unprepared, she attracted the carnal attentions of Brutus, the alpha male of the pride. Filled with confusing feelings of fear, pain, embarrassment . . . and pleasure, having no other options, Faith reluctantly submitted to his amorous advances; innocence was sacrificed. And now, one hundred and eight days later, Faith went into labor. Instinctively, she wandered off by herself. She crawled into the brush and gave birth to one frail little cub.

*W*ithin a couple of days, she and her new daughter, Meeka, went in search of her family. Instead of the anticipated warm reception, she and the cub were savagely pounced upon by Brutus. They had arrived at the worst of all possible times. Brutus was in the midst of defending his position of dominance, battling a rival male challenging his authority. Blinded by passion, no one was safe from his wrath.

Perplexed over being attacked by someone she had known and trusted her entire life, using her own body as a shield, Faith fought with all the fury a young mother could muster to protect her beloved child. But, alas, she was too young, too weak and inexperienced to fully safeguard Meeka against the power of an enraged male. Both she and the cub were badly mauled. Gently carrying her damaged child, Faith slunk away into the surrounding savanna.

This brutality, which had been so surreal, almost dreamlike in quality, took only minutes, but seemed to last an eternity. And while the subsequent physical wounds to both mother and child would eventually heal, the emotional scars of abuse cut deeper; the effects would have a lasting impact.

Feeling both ashamed and humiliated, Faith and Meeka's confidence in a safe, predictable universe had been tarnished, replaced with fear—fear and suspicion. Feeling different and alienated from their peers, unwanted, unaccepted, mother and child remained reclusive nomads, invisible outcasts living on the fringe of society.

Shaken to the core of her being, for years after the incident, Faith was filled with an irrational overprotectiveness of her offspring. Every waking hour was tainted by a shameful memory—her inability to defend Meeka during the attack. To assuage her feelings of guilt, she indulged her little girl, allowing her to nurse well into adulthood. Coddled and babied, Meeka remained infantile in many ways. And while Faith had educated her daughter in the art of finding food, hunting game, and avoiding the many dangers of jungle life, the adolescent lioness preferred to be pampered.

Whenever she did not get her way, raising an accusatory voice, Meeka took on the persona of a needy, spoiled only child. "Mommy, if you realllllly love me, you'll play with me now, not later!"

As time passed and the care giving persisted, Faith came to realize no matter how much attention she showered upon her child, no matter the amount of love, food, and nurturing she gave to Meeka, it would never be enough. Working harder and longer hours to provide for her self-centered daughter, and to insure her own survival, Faith's energy and health began to wane.

The pain and remorse she had carried for so long were now becoming twinged with a disconcerting mix of bitterness toward her child's escalating demands. These emotions precipitated new feelings of judgment, shame, and self-condemnation. And the ever-present memories of her childhood betrayal, the nightmarish attack by that bully, Brutus . . . her protector? Someone she had known all her life and trusted? Her baby's father? These conflicted thoughts were filling her with a debilitating, seething rage—a rage that was turned inward, in the form of depression. It seemed sleep was the only place she could flee her destructive emotions . . . her intolerable circumstances.

*O*ne day, while Meeka slumbered, in an attempt to get away from an endless loop of despair, with no destination in mind, Faith meandered the old circuitous pathways leading to her destiny. She ended up at the bank of a nearby lake—aptly named the Lake of Sorrows and Serenity. As usual she discovered there was no escape; wherever she went, her "feelings" tagged along for the ride. While lowering herself to quench an unquenchable thirst, she saw a reflection looking up at her. Much to her surprise and dismay, though recognized, it wasn't her own. The reflection spoke with the all-too-familiar authority of her disapproving "critical parent's voice."

"What happened to you when you were younger was your own fault. . . . A decent mother would not blame others or resent her own child. Get over it and accept that you are now getting exactly what you deserve!"

At that moment, engulfed by the unrelenting weight of responsibility on one hand, and on the other, depressing feelings of impotence, Faith envisioned herself trapped in a downward spiral—a spiral whose painful depths seemed beyond imagination . . . beyond endurance. Her past had become her present. Her present seemed to be leading toward her future—a road of perpetual sorrow. Laden with an overwhelming sense of futility, Faith considered taking her own life. Was this how it was going to end? Suicide?

As she continued contemplating the morbidly alien, yet in a bizarre way, comforting territory of nihilism, ending her misery, a new image rose from the deep, still water. A hair's breath away—so close . . . so distant, she beheld her long-deceased grandmother's visage. She heard her revered grandmother's dulcet voice.

"Faith . . . oh dear Faith. Have I not told you? Do you not remember the words I once spoke? The words of your ancestors, passed on from my mother's mother from one generation to the next? We were not created to lead eternally happy lives. Yes, happiness and joy are part of the plan, but equally important are sadness and grief. There is a balance, a yin and yang to all existence. It is within the space between the two, where the learning of Life's lessons occurs—a place where Love's essence is revealed. Mother Nature says, 'Do not judge. Bless the happiness . . . bless the sadness. Your triumphs become my triumph . . . your rewards become my reward.' Father Creator says, 'I will never bear upon you more than you can endure. For all my child's needs will I supply.' Faith, trust me; all your goals are attainable. Everything is fated to happen for a reason . . . but that reason may not always be revealed in this lifetime."

A surge of energy filled Faith's being. And with that surge she was transformed by a clarifying flash of insight. She silently thought: While Brutus was consumed by his own battle for survival, unconscious as to the consequences of his actions, he knew not what he had done when he had attacked Meeka and me; I now forgive him. Most of the corrosive anger and blame harbored toward Brutus began to vanish. Now thinking about herself, she pondered: if I had known better, perhaps none of this would have happened; I could and would have done better. However, I had no way of predicting the future. Under the circumstances, I did the best I could . . . I now forgive myself. Much of the punishing guilt and shame she had aimed toward her own heart began to dissipate.

With her grandmother's words—Father Creator's words, "Trust me . . . for all my child's needs will I supply . . ." still ringing in her ears, Faith was distracted by a screeching cry from above. She gazed upwards, witnessing Brother Eagle emblazoned by fire—the golden sun on high, outstretched wings riding thermals, soaring through the azure sky. A dying phoenix birth, a chance to live again, lovingly supported by omniscient Sister Wind.

In her enlightened state, impelled by an urge seemingly beyond her control, Faith sauntered off deeper into the bush. Unexpectedly, she came upon a remarkable scene . . . an answer to an unasked question. While lying low to the ground, well-hidden and camouflaged by her tawny coat, Faith observed a lioness performing a rite of passage ritual with some cubs who were a year or so younger than Meeka.

Because this pride's population had expanded beyond the land's capacity to sustain its members, Jungle law dictated these young adult cubs separate from their family—that they find their own way in the world. The intent of this ritual, performed with both patience and tenderness, had nothing to do with abandonment or avoiding responsibility; but rather the symbolic severing of the umbilical cord of the past—the emotional ties that codependently chained parent to child. This final act of love, a mother's sacrifice, enabled the participants to find true happiness and fulfillment as strong, independent spirits.

*I*nspired by what she had just witnessed, Faith formulated a plan. She'd perform her own ceremony to propel Meeka into a life of self-sufficiency. For several days and nights, accompanied by her rebellious child, Faith tracked the group of newly liberated young lions. Over her muted protests, Meeka was compelled to observe and absorb their behavior patterns as they learned the ropes of foraging on their own. From a safe distance, without explaining why, Faith lectured her daughter on the complex and mystifying topic of tribal protocol, the proper etiquette a young lioness needed to gain peer respect—how to survive within a communal setting.

On the chosen day of initiation, Faith was filled with misgivings. She and her child had shared a lifetime. Their identities were so intertwined, who would she be once her little girl was no longer by her side? How should she act with only her own welfare to think of? What new challenges would await her vulnerable daughter?

Fighting new fears and old demons from the past, she knew this was a task, which must be accomplished. She enticed Meeka to participate in a game. She instructed her offspring to sit quietly, close her eyes, and count to one hundred. Always ready to be the focus of attention and to be entertained, Meeka eagerly obeyed. Faith used her right paw, to draw a circle surrounding her daughter, symbolic of intuition. In her naiveté, unaware of what was about to transpire, her unsuspecting child continued counting. Faith now used her left paw to draw a second circle, symbolic of logic.

*A*s her dearest darling sat at the center of a circle within a circle, Mother Earth's protective arms, Faith purred, "You are a much-loved child, a protected child, a smart child, a strong child, a brave child, a warrior child. And I rename you Courage. You are a much-loved child, a protected child, a smart child, a strong child, a brave child, a warrior child. And I rename you Courage." Over and over Faith repeated these powerful affirmational truths. As she chanted, taking her own words to heart, she realized this rite of passage was, indeed, serving a duel purpose. While her child was being liberated from the parent, she, herself, was simultaneously being freed of her offspring.

Filled with love and compassion, and an uplifting feeling she had not experienced in years; emotions of resentment, guilt and shame faded from consciousness. Faith backed away one step. Repeating her words of praise, she backed away two steps . . . three steps . . . four steps.

Leaving behind forever her damaged spirit, Faith knew from the depth of her soul that the courage to forgive and let go—her trust in an all-loving, protective Mother Nature—call it inner strength, providence, call it God's Will if you must—would carry both her and Meeka into the blissfully fulfilling lives they both deserved. With a much-lightened heart, fortified by hope and grace, Faith dashed off prepared—ready to face whatever the future might bring.

Despite a lingering self-doubt, before too long, Faith found a new family of lions, which accepted her unconditionally. Throughout the years, she gave birth to several litters of cubs. With each new litter, at the time of their rite of passage, Faith would lovingly think of Meeka, her firstborn. As she initiated her latest brood of young adult children, sitting at the center of a circle within a circle, counting to one hundred with their eyes tightly shut; validating their true identities, Faith repeated a familiar life-enhancing, character-building mantra.

"You are a much-loved child, a protected child, a smart child, a strong child, a brave child, a warrior child. And I rename you Courage. You are a much-loved child, a protected child, a smart child, a strong child, a brave child, a warrior child . . . and I proudly rename you Courage. . . . Courage. . . . Courage."

Once again, filled with her own love-inspired courage, Faith took one final step backward—a giant leap forward. She glanced over her shoulder one last time, gazing upon her children—her legacy. And while hearing a celestial song, "As a rainbow follows rain, a lily blooms each spring, a forgiving heart knows joy not pain—a new beginning, innocence reclaimed," Faith bolted into the jungle . . . returning to her pride.

Begin to be now what you will be hereafter.
—William James

Part II
Our Journey With Faith

*Forgive them their trespasses, for they know not
what they do . . . and all too often, neither do we—ELG*

What Was Faith's Journey Telling Us?

By no stretch of the imagination, Faith's journey is everyone's journey. We all carry within our psyches a wounded child, a part of us, which needs to be made whole. Who among us has not been hurt by someone we trusted? All too often white lies, distorted ego needs, betrayals (and even that well-intentioned messenger we metaphorically kill for bearing factual information about something we don't wish to hear), could end what may have been decades of a near-perfect relationship between friends, lovers or family members; so much for the myth about unconditional love. While innocence may be bliss, in a flash of insightful truth, our view of the world and how we define ourselves, may be forever changed.

In the extreme, physical, emotional, and sexual abuse may deprive us of the love and joy we need; robbing us of our innocence, leaving in its wake despair, loneliness and alienation—symptoms of the "walking wounded." Yet, on the other side of the coin, if the truth be told, to a lesser or greater extent, we have all played the roles of both victim and victimizer. More often than we are willing to admit, confusion, anger and frustration may have impelled us to act impulsively, precipitating bad choices and naughty behavior. In the heat of passion or pure stupidity we have all said or done things we regret, hurting the people we honestly love . . . and ultimately, hurting ourself in the process.

In the dance of life, a heart burdened with unresolved anger has no room for a present or future with joy—ELG

However, in spite of what may have occurred, no matter the suffering we may have endured, there is a spark of resiliency lying deep within each of our beating hearts—a hope against hope. That spark says: I want to be happy, healthy and free to laugh, sing and dance with a lightness of spirit. But the rationalizing, excuse making "Doubting Thomas" in our analytical mind asks: How can I achieve these goals with the cards I've been dealt? And with my history, do I deserve to have joy in my life? Unaware that the joy we desire from the depth of our soul is often possible when given the necessary tools and a big helping of elbow grease, we frequently experience the sting of defeat before we even attempt to rise above our present state of affairs.

Feeling like an outsider, different from everyone else, with a nostalgic twinge of jealousy many contemplate: If only I could release my burden, free myself from the school of hard knocks, which is my life; I could stand tall with head held high and be content like everyone else.

We are all full of weakness and errors; let us mutually pardon each other our follies—Voltaire

Forgiveness Hint: *In so-comparing ourselves to others, regardless of ones public mask of contentment, from kings to international celebrities . . . to billionaires, there is not a person amongst us who has not suffered from his or her own set of unmet needs, disappointments, "bad hair days," traumas, guilt-generating misdeeds, misconceptions and a multitude of issues. In other words, we are not as unique and alone in our misery or failings as we believe. Despite appearances, the grass is not always greener on the other side of the fence. It only seems that way because some seasoned individuals are better actors—better able to hide their true feelings, weaknesses, and shameful behavior than the rest of us. (Or perhaps, they just "water their lawns" more frequently in the eye of public opinion.)*

Ironically, as we've seen on the news or read in National Enquirer-type magazines, the biggest closeted sinners all too often appear to be our so-called pillars of society and religious role models. As it turns out, those who are the most dogmatically vocal and mean-spirited in their judgments usually are the most neurotic and unstable in their own private lives. When the spotlight of truth (if not strategically placed Paparazzi cameras) catches them literally or figuratively with their own pants down in the midst of their hypocritical shenanigans, those "flawed pillars with feet of clay," apologize profusely, cry the loudest and beg for the forgiveness they would not grant others.

*By changing our attitude about what has been, we
can increase the possibilities of what can and will be.*
—ELG

As Faith discovered, and her journey illustrates, regardless of what may have happened to us, ultimately, there can be hope for a brighter tomorrow. Faith was able to ignite that spark and heal her wounds through the act of forgiveness. She realized it was a vital component, which guides us back to the "yellow brick road of innocence." Having free will, she chose not to remain a prisoner of the circumstances surrounding her past. Instead of dwelling on what was or what might have been and ending her life, Faith elected to face and live life on her own terms. In crossing a threshold and putting an end to her suffering through right action, she was able to immerse herself in the blessings at hand and bathe herself in optimistic visions of a future filled with promise.

Regarding forgiveness, Ralph Waldo Emerson once said: "For every minute you are angry, you lose sixty seconds of happiness. . . ." If we are inspired by the courage Faith exhibited in facing and overcoming her demons, learning by her example, we no longer need to waste precious minutes, hours, days, years and even decades being unhappy. It is possible for us to take the necessary steps to free ourselves from the painful chains of the past. Like Faith, through forgiveness, we too can travel the path that leads to a bright, joyful future . . . a life we can be proud of and cherish.

An unforgiving heart is forever broken—ELG

What Motivated Faith To Forgive Brutus
For His Unprovoked Attack?

In Faith's journey back to innocence—back to wholeness, knowing it was for her very survival, she needed to transform her core sadness into something positive . . . something constructive. Faith's decision to forgive Brutus was the ultimate answer to her prayers. First and foremost, Faith realized her desire to pardon Brutus had nothing to do with him. Let me repeat: Faith's desire to pardon her abuser had nothing to do with him. The sole (soul) purpose of forgiving the one who had hurt her was entirely for her own sake . . . for her own peace of mind.

Regardless of where he now was living or how Brutus felt about his misdeeds . . . or whether he even thought about them or her at all was of little consequence. Faith's liberating act of forgiveness was an opportunity to put her feelings of shame, guilt, inadequacy, anger and fear in perspective—to reclaim the self-acceptance, self-respect, and self-love lying dormant, but never completely lost . . . a chance to restore a zest for life and peace of mind, which was her true nature.

As an empowered warrior, Faith no longer feared Brutus or anyone else. Instead of being bitter about her ordeal, she actually felt energized by her newly-recognized inner strength. Even though Brutus had victimized and hurt her to the very essence of her being, having outgrown the need to play the blame game or portray the "attention-seeking pity-party" role of martyr, in a strange way Faith could have compassion and even feel sorry for Brutus. He was pathetic. Filled with insecurity, functioning on automatic pilot, he was acting out the fear-based survivalist script life had taught him to play.

To forgive is the highest, most beautiful form of love.
In return, you will receive untold peace and happiness.
—Robert Muller

*I*nsightfully, Faith finally realized while his behavior toward her was inappropriate, unwarranted, and painful to endure; it was reactionary and stupid, not maliciously premeditated. Blinded by rage, Brutus knew not what he had done. Had he known better, if he, himself, had not experienced violence in his past, or if he had learned the lesson of impulse control—to look before you leap, which obviously he had not, he might have acted differently. But lacking the social skills (a hostage of his own inadequacies like the rest of us), Faith now realized, Brutus had done the best he could.

If Brutus would have ever appeared and asked for clemency, without hesitation, Faith would have said, "Yes, I forgive you." And then she'd add: "But more importantly, can you forgive yourself?" As Faith now comprehended, whether victim or victimizer, if we don't search for the causes of our behavior, take responsibility, make amends when possible, and change our ways; asking for forgiveness is useless.

After years of suffering, since Faith, herself, now knew better . . . and knew she deserved better, she took a stand; she refused to carry the burden of Brutus' unconscious, but vile just the same, actions any longer. Replacing hopelessness with hopefulness—self-hatred with self-love, unlike Brutus, who more than likely was still caught up in an unconscious time-warp of denial, Faith could now heal her wounds, leave behind a painful past, and march onward with pride and dignity.

Through forgiveness, the "victim of yesterday" is transformed into today's Triumphant Survivor—ELG

Forgiveness Hint: *Faith comprehended "knowing better," really, really, reallllly knowing better viscerally, not just intellectually in ones mind, is synonymous with "doing better." And actions do speak louder than words when it comes to knowing better.*

The Buddha is alleged to have said: "Holding onto anger is like grasping a hot coal with the intent of throwing it at someone else; you are the one who gets burned." (And Faith realized, holding onto guilt and shame is a decision to throw that hot coal at your own heart.) With this in mind, though she'd never again trust nor want to have anything to do with him, having freed herself of any thoughts of revenge, Faith could now absolve Brutus, "The Bully" for his brutality. However, for self-protection she would always remember him in terms of his misconduct and the impact it had on her life. Free of malice or shame, once again, she reminded herself that forgiving Brutus his trespasses was not for his sake, but rather her gain—to insure her own welfare.

A quote of mine, personifying Faith's call to action, says: "If it doesn't hurt enough or bring enough reward, there's no incentive to change." It seems, since Faith remained stagnating in her emotional tsunami for so long, her "needs to be punished" were being met—it wasn't "hurting enough." Though it would have been better to make the necessary changes earlier . . . changes made for the right reasons, the reward—finding true love and happiness, like many, she had to first hit rock-bottom. It was her core pain that finally propelled her to take action—that compelled her to forgive Brutus and take the necessary steps to escape the prison of sadness she had created. (As they say, "Better late than never." In too many cases, waiting too long has cost abuse victims their lives.)

Before we can forgive one another, we have to understand one another—Emma Goldman

Why Do Some People Do Bad Things That Hurt Others?
How Can This Information Help Us In Our Own Healing?

In the present moment, we are always dealing with what I call "cause and defect." Sadly, all too often we "civilized human beings" lie, steal, cheat on our spouses, abuse others and ourselves. Yet, behind every unkind, illegal, or immoral act, no matter how minor or heinous the offense, there is to be found a logical reason for our transgressions. Hiding behind a façade of authentic or inauthentic cluelessness, we are often driven to distraction, if not, delinquency, by self-deluded thoughts of ego-enhancement, greed, power, revenge or untamed hormones. Though most of us have a conscience, and will feel remorse for our fall from grace, blinded by rationalizing defense mechanisms and ambition, some deranged narcissists surmise, they can get away with their unsavory acts unscathed. But they are mistaken. Somewhere down the road there is a piper to be paid.

At one time or another we have all lied about something. Aside from manipulation for financial, personal or "erotic" gain, there are three other reasons we fib. First there is the "white lie" used to spare another's feelings. We tell our beloved wife, "Your pot roast was delicious," when in fact, it tasted like cardboard. At times, we act deceptively to protect the outer mask of self, our own ego (or butt) from the judgment of others. Something we did or said might have a negative impact, which could cost us love, respect, friendship, a job, money or even our freedom should the truth be known. "No, Officer, I haven't been drinking. That empty beer bottle you found in my car is for the recycling center." And a third reason we are dishonest or exaggerate the facts "just a little," is to impress others, inflate our ego—to gain unearned respect or envy among our peers.

Those who invalidate others to validate themselves,
invalidate themselves by exposing their insecurities—ELG

A *"Great Gatsby" persona can open doors and gain us perks that accompany being viewed as someone with money, power or status. "Yeah, I'll be flying to Paris with my supermodel girlfriend to see the Louvre. Then we'll return to my home in the Hamptoms for a private concert with Madonna...." (Are you impressed?)*

Besides being habitual liars, some may just plain out-and-out steal from us. Perhaps as kids, they were neglected. Now, out of anger and an inflated sense of entitlement, these bottomless pits of neediness just take what they want. At times, a man may cheat on his wife, believing sex to be the proving ground of his self-worth. A wife might feel unappreciated by her spouse, finding it exciting to get the love she's missing at home in the arms of a stranger. (Or perhaps, all these defective behaviors resulted from a dysfunctional family that taught distorted family values.)

Speaking of dysfunctional families, when dealing with issues of child (or spousal) abuse, the majority of offenders were, themselves, victims of abuse. They imprinted on what we might label "perverted behavior patterns" that are often carried into their adult lives. (As distorted as these adaptive and often irreversible coping mechanisms may be, lest we forget, they were the only tools these "once innocent children" had to survive in a sea of uncertainty, pain, and fear.) Having been victimized as children, if they have not sought professional help and/or done the necessary inner work to heal their wounds, as adults, they are often predisposed to abusing children, themselves. And if they don't hurt children, these sociopathic bullies, might take out their rage on almost anyone they can intimidate.

For better or worse, childhood sculpts us into the adults we must deal with today—ELG

*S*ince their caregivers failed to show them love at the time they needed it the most, distorted by their experiences, abusers often lack compassion for anyone else. From a position of weakness not strength, lacking a conscience and appropriate boundaries (something we are not born with—something that must be taught, developed and nurtured in early childhood), they are driven to excess. They may shield themselves from further pain by psychologically wearing protective armor, being manipulative and controlling. Feeling powerless as children, they now need to lord it over others and often employ the most ruthless of tactics to get those needs met. While presenting a daring façade of invincibility, even some of those we recognize as our authority figures and successful "captains of industry," in actuality, may be hiding and at times expressing an inner rage associated with their victimhood, overcompensating for true feelings of vulnerability.

However, not all victims of abuse will hurt others. Some may internalize their feelings, hurting themselves, instead. Having developed a distorted self-concept, a belief they deserve to be mistreated, they may exhibit a lifelong behavior of attracting unhealthy relationships, which re-enforce and perpetuate their victimization. Being unable to trust others motives, it's common for damaged beings to routinely sabotage healthy relationships with decent companions who could have made them happy. Other victims of abuse, feeling paranoically defenseless, withdraw into their own world, isolating themselves in a loveless sea of fear, sadness and alienation. (On a more uplifting note, some inspiring, kind-hearted souls, having risen above their own painful experiences, will dedicate their lives helping others to do the same.)

Through free will we can choose to remain a victim wallowing in anger—imprisoned by fear and self-pity, or we can choose victory, peace of mind, and self-love—ELG

While most abusers were physically and psychologically traumatized as children, there are other causes for both extreme and less severe, "run-of-the-mill" defective behavior. Some individuals may have genetic abnormalities or physically damaged nervous systems of known or unknown origins. They might suffer from bipolar-like chemical imbalances, and/or drug and alcohol addictions, which can lead to impaired judgment, impulse control issues, and antisocial activities. Lacking common sense or proper social graces (or intelligence), at times, we humans just say or do things out of our own ignorance, unaware we are inadvertently hurting another's feelings. And finally, some of us, motivated by our insecurities, jealousy and/or out of anger may act premeditatedly, seeking revenge in a misguided attempt to right a wrong. (Believe me while revenge might bring us temporary satisfaction, it never gives us peace of mind; it never heals our wounds. In fact, attempting to "get even," in the long run, often has the opposite effect of increasing our pain and making matters worse.)

Even though all the above-mentioned are valid reasons for inappropriate conduct, as we may sadly know from our own personal experience, aberrant behavior causes innocent people to suffer. However, it is important to remember, that our forgiveness does by no means excuse the abuser's behavior or release him or her from the responsibility and consequences of their actions. To help safeguard all of us from dangerous renegades, Society and most religions demand that victimizers pay a legal and moral price for their crimes and misdemeanors—Society's way to protect herself from the "defects" of others regardless of the causes.

*To forgive is to set a prisoner free and discover
the prisoner was you—Louis B. Smedes*

Forgiveness Hint: *Remember, we are all born innocent, so as we now know, there are reasons why some people hurt others. When attempting to forgive an abuser or someone who failed to live up to our expectations (or ourself), it may be useful to ask and answer these five questions:*

1. *Was it the abuser's fault he or she grew up in a dysfunctional and/or abusive family, leaving them with unmet needs and low self-worth? "No!"*
2. *Was it their fault they had a damaged, reactive nervous system and impulse control issues? "No!"*
3. *Was it their fault they had a chemical imbalance or inherited a physiological predisposition for addictive behavior? "No!"*
4. *Was it their fault, they lacked common sense and unintentionally hurt our feelings? "No!"*
5. *Is it their fault they may continue to hurt others intentionally and seem unremorseful? A tough one to accept, but the answer is "No!" Devoid of the tools to conquer their demons or ego deficiencies; like a leopard unable to change his spots, many are just too physically or emotionally damaged, unenlightened or dimwitted and therefore, incapable of changing their pathological ways.*

While none of the above justifies bad behavior, it does enhance our understanding of why some humans hurt each other. (And if we'd been terrorized as kids or had some of the above issues, we too may have devolved into serial offenders or perennial victims.) Following Faith's lead, we can remind ourselves that we are forgiving these damaged beings, Society's misfits, entirely for our own sake. We can facilitate our own healing and protect ourselves from further trauma by considering the cause of our abusers defective actions, while still remembering and holding them accountable for their conduct.

While silence may be golden and sometimes speaks louder than words, actions speak loudest of all—ELG.

How Was Faith Able To Forgive And Rid Herself Of The Self-punishing Judgments Carried In Her Heart And Mind? How Can We Begin To Forgive Ourselves?

At her lowest point Faith realized as long as she viewed herself as a victim, by allowing her "critical parent's voice"—any negative voice in her head, to mentally assault her with guilt-trips and shame, her anger and misery would continue to escalate. Subsequently, these obsessive, energy-draining, self-defeating mindsets would continue to negatively impact her life both emotionally and physically. While in some ways she could forgive Brutus as part of the formula for healing, unexpectedly, forgiving herself seemed more problematic, but just as essential. The first thing she did was to stop that critical parent's voice in its tracks by calling it what it was . . . a liar—a liar she no longer needed to listen to. Instead, Faith contemplated her own voice—the truth:

"Hindsight being 20/20, what happened to me was only partially my fault. And I claim responsibility for that. Perhaps, if I'd been more aware, the attack might have been avoided. But the facts remain, I was simply at the wrong place at the wrong time. Due to circumstances beyond my control, at one time I was victimized. But being victimized does not automatically make me a victim for life nor do I need to define myself as such. Playing the role of the 'impotent walking wounded' is a choice; it is something I now vehemently reject! In fact, because of my trauma, I am now a much stronger being—stronger than most who have never been tested."

Life's only constant is the unpredictability of change—ELG

Forgiveness Hint: *Accepting the fact none of us are born perfect—we all have flaws and occasionally screw up, is a big step toward our own "attitude adjustment." No one amongst us can safely disarm a land mine, fly an airplane, or climb Mount Everest, unless we have been taught how to perform the task, have the right tools, and are prepared. Despite the claims of her critical parent's voice, Faith recognized her past inadequacies, pains, disappointments, and reactive emotions associated with her trauma should remain filed in memory as something that once happened to the person she was then—a mere child who lacked the self-protective insights and skills she now had as a mature adult. Smarter and wiser, she understood those experiences helped to sculpt her into the fierce lioness she had become. As a result of self-acceptance and a desire to learn new survival techniques, with this improved confidence based on increased competence, Faith found it possible to have a secure, fulfilling, and happy life, shortcomings and all.*

Survival dictates we do the best we can with the cards we've been dealt—even when those cards are inadequate, fail to conform to Society's norm and routinely lead to pain and chaos for everyone sitting at the table. If we wish to improve our lot in life, we must reshuffle the deck. Knowing there are causes for our own inadequacies and defective behavior makes it easier to change our wayward ways, silence our critical parent's voice, and forgive ourself, as well as others. With a new attitude, the physical and residual emotional scars we may bear from any abusive situation can be proudly claimed as evidence we no longer see ourselves as victims. On the contrary, claiming victory, like Faith, we can convert an inferior hand into a full house, and emphatically decree: "I AM A WINNER IN THE GAME OF LIFE!"

The acid of hate destroys the container that holds it.
—An Amish Saying

How Was Faith Able To Free Herself From Her Demanding Cub, Meeka, And Other Baggage That Made Her Unhappy?

By listening to the uplifting words of her deceased grandmother, which effectively dealt with her "critical parent's" irrational and toxic ranting at the Lake of Sorrows and Serenity; Faith found the strength to take responsibility "only where responsibility was due." Finally, after years of suffering with undeserved guilt, she could forgive her abuser and herself regarding her ordeal. Still, she realized in order to progress to the next step in achieving her goals and finding hope for the future, she would now have to free herself from her self-centered, energy-draining cub. As long as Faith carried with her the insatiable needs and emotional liability of Meeka, symbolically another judgmental part of herself, her life would remain an exercise in futility.

As Faith learned, it is our codependent relationship with our "damaged inner child," reinforced by condemnatory voices from our past, which help to perpetuate our victimization. These two elements deplete us of energy and rob us of the joy at hand by arousing our anger, guilt, shame, and feelings of inadequacy—the rationalized excuses for our present day misery, bad choices, and self-destructive behavior.

*There came a time when the risk to remain tight in
the bud was more painful than the risk it took to bloom.*
                                                    —Anais Nin

*F*aith was forced to confront one of her biggest fears—a fear that holds many of us hostage to our past. She asked herself: "Who will I be once I free myself of Meeka and she is no longer by my side?" This frame of mind is like having one foot on our car's accelerator, wanting desperately to escape from conflicted circumstances, which have labeled us a "victim," while having another foot on the brake—neurotically yoking us to that flawed but familiar identity we've learned to embrace and cope with. Rather than face the challenge of an uncertain future—a future where our life may be radically altered, where we will be forced to adjust to an untried yet healthier way of seeing and defining our self; all too often "we keep our foot on the brake." Like Faith, we too may question: Who will I be? Can I survive the change? Ruled by our insecurities, fear keeps us mired in bad situations. It may thwart us in our attempt at making necessary changes—severing our ties to the past and a painful present.

Ultimately Faith discovered she had nothing to fear but fear itself. By metaphorically taking her foot off the brake and putting the pedal to the metal, overcoming her resistance to change, she was lightened of her burden. With an improved self-concept and attitude—a new, empowered persona, Faith was able to release Meeka to her own fate. In having broken that codependent bond to a troubling past, she found true happiness and a heart filled with grace.

Freedom is what we do with what's been done to us.
—Jean-Paul Sartre

Forgiveness Hint: *As we have seen, Faith's liberation was facilitated by her handling of two main issues. She quieted an unwanted mental intruder—that judgmental "critical parent's voice" in her head, calling it what it was—a liar. And she separated from and released her energy-draining, "insatiable inner child," by performing a healing ritual, renaming Meeka, "Courage."*

If we had been Faith, how would we have handled our hurtful, mental voices that seemed to constantly berate and dwell on our shortcomings . . . robbing us of our pride? What kind of a ceremony could we have created to free us of that self-protective, wounded part of us, which now no longer served a constructive purpose?

A ritual that helped me was to write down some of the condemnatory statements I often heard in my head or I spoke to myself out loud—the downloaded voices of my critical parent and needy inner child. I then crumpled the paper, threw it in my fireplace, and as it burned I spoke my truth. Instead of hearing "You're unlovable and stupid; you'll never succeed at anything," I passionately proclaimed out loud: "In fact, I am worthy of being loved! I'm smarter than a lot of people! I have a proven record of success and I am proud of my accomplishments! That is my truth! Critical voice and demanding inner child, I'm now in charge! I no longer allow you in my life! You're nothing but 'mental spam,' an uninvited guest I am deleting, so leave!"

If the negative voices return, as they occasionally do, I simply say out loud: "Stop it! Go away!" Then doing my own programming, uprooting these unwanted mental weeds of discontent, I state the opposite of what was being spewed. Empowered by taking control of my thoughts, I'm free to cultivate a good life–a life filled with poetry and flowers.

Forgive your enemies, but never forget their names.
—John F. Kennedy

What Was Faith's Formula For Leading A Contented, Fulfilling Life After Her Ordeal?

*U*ltimately, Faith came to understand when it comes to a betrayal –abuse, infidelity... anything that someone has done to us (or we may have done to another), it is not a matter of forgiving and forgetting, but rather "forgiving and remembering." Albert Einstein allegedly said: "Insanity is doing the same thing over and over and expecting different results..." What we fail to remember, what we deny or choose to forget, destines us for a repeat performance—a performance, which will always generate the same tragic outcome.

Yet the question arises, if instead of sweeping it under the rug, pretending it never happened, Faith continued to recall her victimization experience, a trauma that broke her heart and bruised her ego; wouldn't the damaging feelings generated from her wounds be kept alive?

On the surface this seems to be the case, but it need not be. Rather than wasting energy on that which could not be changed, Faith was able to adjust her perception of Brutus' attack. She understood strong emotions often blind us to logical thinking, thus precluding us from finding alternate solutions and handling problems effectively. With certainly, Brutus was not thinking clearly when he attacked her and his own daughter. And Faith realized she was not thinking clearly by allowing her emotions to run rampant—restimulating the associative torment that controlled her life each time she thought of Brutus.

An eye for an eye, tooth for tooth mentality leaves every-one eternally blind, hungry for love, and angry—ELG

Our jails are filled with sociopaths, as well as, "nice people" who, like Brutus, let their emotions get the better of them—reactively committing "crimes of passion." Our mental hospitals are filled with patients ruled by their emotions—unable to cope with their victimization or life's other challenges. Intuitively, Faith chose a better path. Instead of denying her painful feelings or letting them rule her life, she embraced them. She recognized they were motivational tools she needed—tools that impelled her to grow and evolve beyond her traumas.

In order to succeed, she changed her perception as to what had occurred in the past. She reframed the emotionally-charged incident with Brutus (including her own oversights that contributed to Meeka's injuries). She began to "analyze and witness the event" as if she were an impartial observer rather than a participant, the "audience rather than the actor." Instead of dwelling on the pain and gory details… the drama she shared with Brutus, Faith objectively focused on the facts (as if one were to write a short synopsis of a play).

For her, these were the facts: "She (the actress) entered the alpha male lion's territory at the wrong time. While from past observations she knew he could be violent, she was unaware of the danger and subsequently was attacked. She defended her cub and herself to the best of her ability. And they survived. Wiser for the experience, she would be more cautious when approaching new and even familiar surroundings. She reminded herself that authentic love is supposed to be uplifting and supportive not painful and destructive. For future reference, she would be more discerning in her relationships, as well."

Living well is the best revenge—George Herbert

In a detached manner, Faith repeated the above account over and over again, until she could honestly claim and own it as her own "downloaded truth"—until she could calmly, in a rational manner internalize the facts of her scripted story . . . and even share them with others in the first person, replacing "she" with "I" with minimal emotional buzz.

Since Faith no longer considered herself a victim, she no longer needed to feel the negative emotions, which accompanied victimhood. By concentrating on the lessons to be found in each experience, instead of mentally beating herself to a pulp over situations beyond her control, through forgiveness and dispassionately witnessing and analyzing episodes in her life impersonally, she could disarm the toxic effects of the abuse. As a result of this new life-affirming attitude, she discovered an increased energy and experienced a vast improvement of both her mental and physical health.

While over time most of Faith's emotional pain and anger faded, some residual scars to her psyche remained. However, having been put in perspective, those relics of her history did not deprive her of her present joy. In actuality, those scars were proudly treasured as self-protective reminders she had conquered her fears. Instead of being saddled with sadness, Faith was uplifted by the knowledge that having paid her dues and having adjusted her life accordingly, she could claim her power. She had learned her lessons well. These insights allowed her to break old destructive patterns and avoid any further instant replays of situations that caused suffering.

*Forgiveness saves the expense of anger, the cost
of hatred, and the waste of spirit—Hannah More*

(**Forgiveness Hint:** *The process of first feeling her feelings and then using her discomfort as a motivational tool, the catalyst needed for changing her perceptions of past occurrences, allowed Faith to manage life's demands more effectively. In essence, mirroring the writings of the ancient Roman philosopher, Boethius, Faith began to live her life one day at a time. Enjoying one moment at a time, she now recognized hardships as a pathway to liberation—a pathway to peace. She accepted that which could not be changed, the past; she changed that which could be changed, her attitude about the past, as well as proven unhealthy practices. In forgiving and accepting herself, acknowledging her challenges without condemnation or judgment, and analyzing each new experience with an open mind; Faith gained the strength and wisdom to proactively ward off potential problems. Unhampered by inner conflicts and feelings of shame or blame, she could claim her true identity and engage in constructive, self-affirming behaviors.*

As Faith demonstrated, by minimizing the emotional component of past events, viewing each encounter as an opportunity for growth—"opportunities in work clothes," we too can break destructive patterns that may have plagued and handicapped us. Using Faith's "objectified story" as an example, if we were to write a short outline or script documenting our own experience, told from the perspective we were witnessing it happen to someone else, ie., "She did this . . . and he did that," what would be the facts . . . the life-enhancing lessons learned? (Along these lines, upon occasion, I've drafted and then rewritten letters I have no intention of sending to the people who hurt me. I've found seeing my thoughts out-pictured on paper and reading them several times to be another safe, non-confrontational way to express, objectify, tame and heal my emotions.)

When a humbled heart listens, angels sing a healing song of love—ELG.

Summary Of What Faith's Journey Has Shared

As Faith has shown, whether someone we trusted lied, cheated on a relationship, picked our pocket, or just plain hurt our feelings; optimistically, we can always have hope for a brighter tomorrow . . . even in those cases of extreme physical, emotional, and sexual abuse. While all of the above may temporarily rob us of the joy we deserve, the good news is, no one can permanently take away our happiness without our permission; healing is possible. Traumas can be restructured and then reinterpreted as important "consciousness-raising experiences," rather than merely "punishments to be endured."

As a result of this shift in perspective, there may a silver lining to our tragedy. The pain caused by a betrayal or trauma often generates a deep sense of empathy for others . . . and a new direction and meaning for ones own life. This might lead to a life of service. Having a purpose helping others in need has often been found to be an effective way of increasing a sense of self-worth, healing despair and depression, and subsequently, generating a sense of fulfillment. (Something I know from personal experience.)

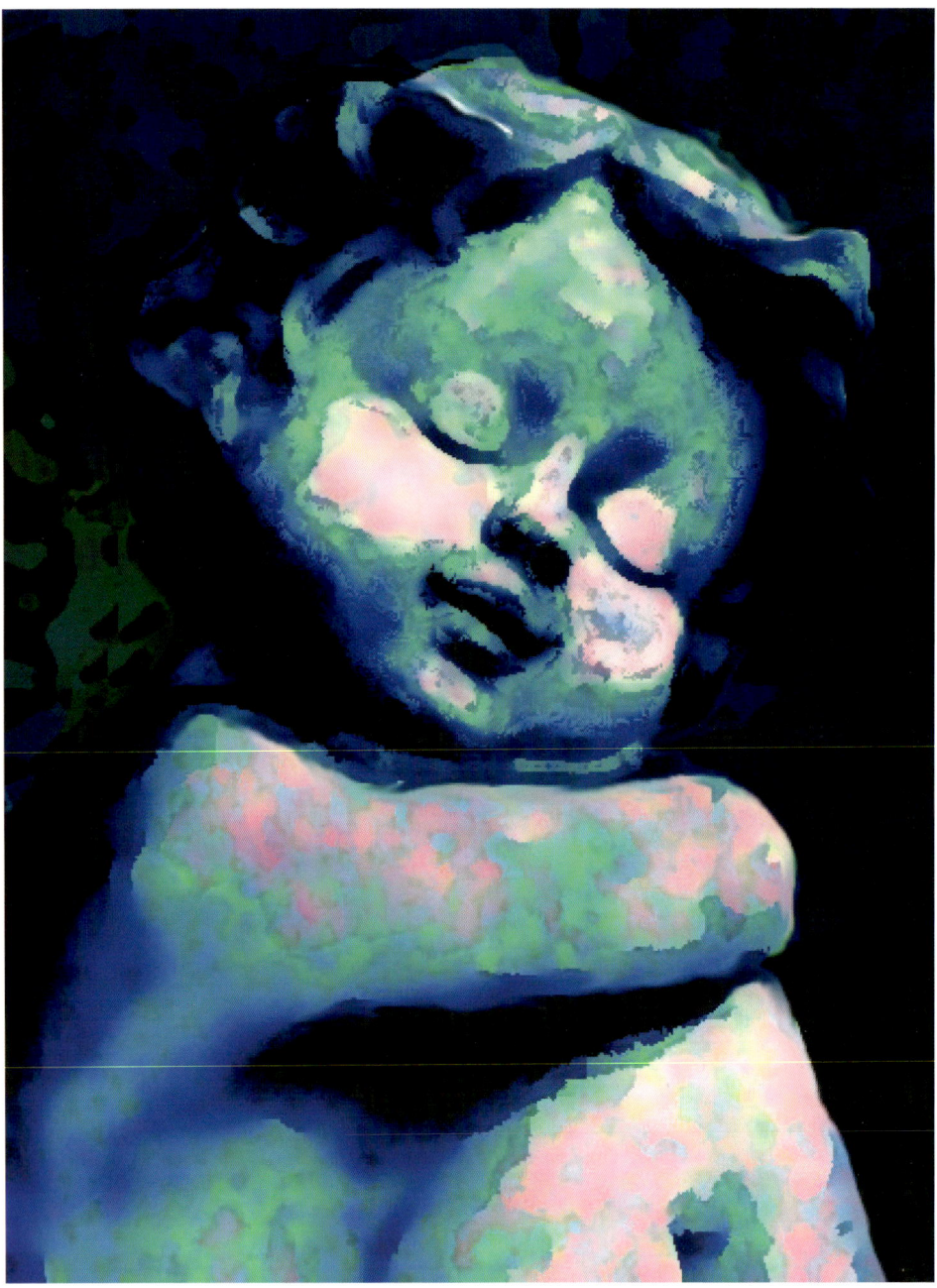

When Love fills all space and we wish everyone well, by releasing all to their own destiny, we remember, recognize and embrace the innocence we always had–ELG

*A*t the very end of Faith's journey, rather than dwelling in anger and rage over the unpleasantness endured, our heroine lioness was filled with love and benevolence. We, ourselves, have a choice. Our own history can generate a similar happy ending by making us better, not bitter. When considering the curve balls life throws at us, we have it within our power to make "sweet nectar out of sour grapes" or we can continue to live off of "bitter herbs," ignoring all the vast fields of delectable, sun-ripened strawberries in our midst. Whether former victim or reformed abuser, if we choose to conquer a challenging past, heal our wounds and claim the harmonious life we were born to have; following Faith's example, we must:

1. Forgive the Perpetrator

   A. Whether our abuser is living, deceased . . . or whether we ever see them again or they know we are forgiving them; forgiving them is entirely for our own peace of mind and physical well-being.

   B. Remember, there are always causes for "defective behavior." Many, but not all abusers were themselves, victimized or neglected as children. And due to a twist of "biological fate," it is not uncommon for some perpetrators to suffer from mental, psychological, neurological and/or biochemical deficiencies.

   C. While we forgive the perpetrator, legally and morally, they must still be held accountable for their transgressions.

Wishing you a new beginning of peace, love, and joy.
—Edward Lee Goldstein

2. *With Compassion Forgive Ourself*
   A. Knowing we did the best we could with the skills we possessed at the time of our ordeal, we accept no one is perfect—to err is human, screw-ups are inevitable. Without magnifying our blame or shame, we assume responsibility "only where responsibility is due." We then silence that lying, bullying "critical parent's voice." Finally, we take charge of our inner thoughts and outer spoken words, by diligently performing our own uplifting, self-worth generating mental reprogramming.
   B. Release our "damaged inner child"—another judgmental part of ourself, to its own destiny.
   C. And while we're at it, weed from our life all those invalidating, subversive, so-called friends and family members who continue to emotionally abuse us. Create new relationships and socialize only with people who show us love and respect.

3. *Forgive and Remember*
   A. What we fail to remember we're destined to repeat. So instead of denying our feelings, feel and embrace them as motivators for action and change—future signposts of potential danger to be avoided.
   B. Objectify and distance ourself from the trauma by focusing on the life-enhancing, strengthening lessons learned in each experience.
   C. When we do recall our experience, proudly own our scars as evidence of our fortitude.

4. *As victors in the game of life, reclaim our true identity—our innocence, by authentically smiling and affirming out loud for the entire world to see and hear: "I am much-loved! I am protected, smart, strong, and a brave warrior. And yes, above all else: I AM A JOY-FILLED, COURAGEOUS SURVIVOR!"*

*F*aith gained many insights on her journey and internalized these healing truths: when we forgive our enemies, we no longer have any enemies. When we forgive our self, we become our own best friend. Instead of seeing toxic anger and hate, a new and improved Faith could examine the fabric of her life and honestly say, "My heart is pure." If we are willing, we can discover what Faith learned along the way. The only wizard to be found on this adventure we called "lessons on forgiveness" is our own unbounded courage, clarity of mind, and heartfelt pureness of spirit . . . in other words, our true identity.

In our own enlightened state, we too can now have compassion for everyone—compassion even for those who consciously or unconsciously attempted to harm us. Above all else, we can have compassion for ourself. Like Faith, we can now look at ourself in the mirror and be proud to speak our truth out loud:

> "Despite What Happened In The Past,
> Despite My Present Circumstances,
> Despite What Others Told Me About Myself,
> Despite What I Now Think Of Myself,
> I AM INNOCENT! We ARE ALL INNOCENT!
> AND YES! I LOVE ME! I LOVE AND
> ACCEPT ME, MYSELF AND I . . . AS I AM!"

And with this last task, sustained by our newly-rediscovered inner strength, we have finally completed our healing journey shared with Faith. Welcome home my courageous friend . . . welcome back to innocence.

Epilogue

Final Thoughts On Faith's Legacy

Some time ago, a woman named Mary, who had read my autobiography, The Male Thing Explained, phoned to thank me for writing, "Such an insightfully honest, entertaining and educational book." She went on to say, "As a little girl, I had been abused by a relative and the scars have never healed. But reading your book brought out my 'damaged inner child' for the first time in my life with feelings of love and compassion rather than my usual anger and rage. . . ."

I'm always elated when my reading and lecture audience report my words have been a catalyst for healing in their lives . . . and I have received many such responses. However, this particular reader was not quite finished with her thoughts. She continued, "Yes, that 'damaged inner child' was brought out with love and compassion, but as you must know, no matter how much attention, sex, drugs, alcohol or food you feed your 'damaged inner child,' it's never enough. . . ."

Being an empath, having an exaggerated ability to feel other's feelings, my elation turned to sadness over Mary's broken spirit. In my forty years as a health educator, physical therapist and forgiveness expert, I've worked with thousands of clients. Years ago I came to realize, many of us have spent a lifetime being codependent on our damaged inner child, using it as an excuse for our present day miseries. I've counseled many women and men who were wounded by child and/or spousal abuse. Most of them have a strong aura of depression, which they wear on their persona as a badge of victimhood. This bearing of defeat overshadows and, in some ways, undermines their boastful claim, "I'm a survivor!"

Since it is our damaged inner child, which defines and confines us to the past, while some may see themselves as "survivors," which they may well be . . . they are unhappy survivors. I suggest to my clients to do what I have done: "Give up that 'damaged inner child' for adoption." I lovingly thanked him for the years of protection he afforded me; I blessed him for the lessons he shared and then released him to his destiny. In so-doing, lightened of a tremendous source of woe, which had been plaguing me for decades, I discovered I could open a new chapter in my life. With no more excuses, or the blaming of parents, siblings, teachers, friends or foes who scarred or scared me—who had wittingly, unwittingly, or "dim-wittingly" betrayed my trust and innocence, I was truly enlightened. In reclaiming my innocence, there were no more victims or victimizers. I could finally discover my "undamaged, healthy inner child," which had been hiding in my psyche all these years, patiently waiting for me to grow up.

Born of my conversation with Mary, the idea for *Faith—A Lion's Healing Journey Back to Innocence* was conceived. It would be pretentious to say, "I wrote Faith's story," since the story just poured out of me, as did an infinitude of repressed tears. Faith's journey literally wrote itself through me. In the process, I found this truth: A well-earned happiness—the sunshine of self-love blossoms only when we cultivate both a greater self-acceptance as well as an increased tolerance of others' imperfections. It is my deepest desire Faith's story—all our stories inspire my readers "to give their own damaged inner child up for adoption . . . inviting their 'joy-filled healthy inner child' to come out to play."

Much playfulness coming your way,

Edward Lee Goldstein

P.S. I recently saw an interview with Jacee Dugard, author of *A Stolen Life*. She was kidnapped at age 11, held captive for eighteen years and brutalized in every demeaning way imaginable. She escaped her tormentors at the age of twenty-nine. When asked about her feelings toward her abusers, she said she was not going to victimize herself by dwelling on them. Reclaiming her innocence, she said they were disturbed people who did terrible things, but she, herself, did nothing wrong. She refused to give them the power to ruin her life. Despite the circumstances of their birth, Jacee was even grateful for the blessings of her two daughters (one born when she was only 13 years old). She said they made life bearable and taught her about unconditional love. . . .

Now that's what I'd call a woman who really understands forgiveness—a triumphant survivor. May courageous Jacee Dugard inspire us all on our own healing journey.

The journey from victim to victory begins with the desire to heal. It succeeds when we have the faith and courage to take the only step necessary . . . we nurture a forgiving heart.
—ELG

Appendix A

Evolution Of The Damaged Inner Child And Critical Parent

We accept a baby is born innocent, but it's hard for us to admit that as adults, we fall short of perfection and all have "oops" moments. "Darn it!" Why do we sit in such harsh judgment of ourselves and others? Where did that "damaged inner child" and "critical parent's voice" come from? Assuming our infant is healthy, with a normal nervous system, at birth he possesses a very selfish and demanding inner child—selfish, but "undamaged." That self-centered little angel's demands revolve around his biological needs, such as: adequate food, a warm, clean bed . . . a gentle touch. His very survival depends on these basic needs being addressed.

For his first two years of life, an infant is in a constant state of openness, downloading data, mimicking Mom's smile, when she smiles; feeling distress if Dad's angry. Through observing those inhabiting his world and their responses to his behavior, as time passes, the child learns the basic ropes about what's considered appropriate behavior and that which is inappropriate. If he's been blessed with loving custodians who always fulfill his needs, he'll develop a secure self-concept, a healthy inner child who feels: "This is a safe, friendly, supportive world." Contrariwise, if his cries for help go unheeded and he's spanked just because his parents are in a foul mood, he's imprinting: "This is a dog-eat-dog world! Nobody cares about me, so why should I care about anyone else?" He will then grow up feeling insecure, with a damaged inner child—a distorted sense of self and unmet entitlement needs. In the extreme the abused or neglected child fails to develop a conscience and may devolve into that sociopath who takes what he wants without remorse.

Surprisingly, attitudes of guilt and shame are an important component for the creation of a healthy, socially-acceptable human being. They're also responsible for the birth of our critical parent's voice. It is through the "scarring of our psyche" we learn to conform as civilized members of our culture. In reality, just as much as love shapes our identity, guilt and shame teach us how to modify, control and inhibit the behaviors our parents and Society deem offensive or immoral. Once an infant begins to link language with feelings of joy and sadness—with approving or disapproving attitudes of his caregivers, guilt and shame are born. How those around us "disapprovingly react" to our "bad behavior" gives birth to and evolves our critical parent's voice and further affects the inner child's sense of self. The maturing toddler's "simple, non-judgmental . . . I can do no wrong ego" that he was born with, now has a conscience—a ruler used to measure what he learns to view as acceptable or unacceptable behavior. For better or worse, this consciousness of right and wrong (or lack of consciousness due to substandard parenting) is what sculpts our sense of identity, how we see the world, and the emotional tone of our personality.

So what does guilt actually represent? Guilt addresses the "disapproval of an action." For example, when a toddler poops in his pants instead of the toilet, his mom might say: "Jonnie, that was a 'bad thing you did'. Pooping in your pants hurts mommy's feelings." In this case, Mom is chastising the "action," not the "actor." Jonnie internalizes, "Pooping in my pants upsets my mommy." Feeling pangs of guilt, that something he does hurts someone he loves, he'll make a conscious effort to improve his potty habits. (Or our "innocent darling" may at times still poop in his pants to get attention, to assert his power, or for passive-aggressive purposes of revenge.)

While guilt is an assault on an action, shame goes for the jugular, attacking the person. When our boy poops in his pants, and Mom, vents: "JONNIE, YOU ARE A BAD BOY! HOW COULD YOU BE SO STUPID!"; when Dad jokes, "WITH THOSE BIG EARS, YOU LOOK LIKE DUMBO THE ELEPHANT!"; they are attacking him personally. Whenever Jonnie has an accident or fails to live up to Mom or Dad's expectations (which he has now internalized as his own download for "appropriate, acceptable behavior," his own identity), he's going to mentally hear their criticizing voices. Becoming his own "judgmental parent," ashamed of not only what he does, but infinitely more damaging, who he is, he's going to attack himself—beat himself up with the same venom aimed at him by his all-knowing role models. "I'M A BAD BOY (for making Mommy angry!) WITH MY BIG EARS, I AM A FREAK! They're right, I FAIL AT EVERYTHING . . . I'M REALLY A JERK!"

There's another factor about the critical parent's voice, which has nothing to do with guilt or shame; it's all about imprinting. When a youngster witnesses his mom have a hissy fit because she "dropped her mixing bowl," he's seeing her express her own downloaded critical parent. "DAMN IT! HOW COULD I BE SUCH AN IDIOT!!!" At an early age this teaches him to vent his own judgmental voice—to berate and humiliate himself, when he's less than perfect at any task. . . . Sound familiar?

In understanding the damaged inner child and the critical parent, as enlightened adults we can tap into our "healthy inner child" . . . input our own "supportive parent's voice." By replacing old, useless and destructive mental tapes with positive, uplifting, ego-enhancing programing; with a bit of hope, faith and due diligence, we can become the balanced, joyful person we deserve to be.

Appendix B
To Forgive, Or Not Forgive: That Is The Question

In Faith's journey, we spoke of the importance of forgiving others and ourself. Aside from some psychological factors, as we shall see later, there are a number of significant health benefits associated with releasing emotions that negatively affect our lives. In seeming contradiction, holding onto anger and withholding forgiveness, at times, may seem warranted.

Justifications For Withholding Forgiveness

1. If our pain is too great and we're truly vulnerable, holding onto our emotional scars, delaying forgiveness until we're stronger may protect us from further trauma.
2. To prevent future offenses or to capitalize off someone else's weakness, rather than forgiving, verbally or physically venting our outrage can intimidate the "enemy"—a way to assert dominance, maintain power, conceal our own weaknesses. (Preserving someone's status as "the enemy" may give moral justification for retaliation.)
3. "Conditional forgiveness" may be in the best interest of the "sinner." He's destined to repeat his offences, until he's learned to take responsibility and paid the monetary, moral or emotional price for his wicked ways.
4. Sometimes people will try to manipulate us with guilt to forgive them—deflecting their bad behavior by blaming us. "Yeah, I know I cheated once, . . . OK, twice. But divorce? Look what you're doing to the children!"
5. Milking the role of the "self-righteous victim" gets us attention . . . and sometimes sympathy or guilt inspires others to "lick our wounds"—to give us that "much-needed diamond ring"— in essence, buying our forgiveness. (But in reality, secondary gains for being wounded can also reinforce and perpetuate the "victim mentality.")

Considerations To Inspire Forgiveness

1. *Related to stress and anger are symptoms of anxiety, frustration, depression, passive/aggressive attacks on others and ourself—being accident prone and even feeling suicidal.*

2. *There are significant health related issues, as well. Even short bursts of anger can increase our blood pressure or cause a fatal heart attack or paralyzing stroke.*

3. *During times of anger or chronic stress, less blood flows to our logical thinking brain, with an increase flow to the emotional, reactionary, survivalist areas. We are literally not thinking clearly, when we're being hijacked by our emotions.*

4. *The chemical cortisol is associated with the "fight or flight" hormone of adrenalin. It impacts our bodies during both acute flare-ups of stress, and sustained episodes of anxiety, fear and anger—symptoms often related to withholding forgiveness. So what does cortisol do?*

A. It increases fat in our blood creating a temporary energy boost to meet a perceived emergency–a good thing.

B. During chronic bouts of stressful emotion, cortisol stores fat in our body as a reserve. This can lead to high blood pressure, clogged arteries, coronary heart disease, and even weight gain—a not so good thing.

C. Our immune system is compromised when we are chronically dealing with stress. Under cortisol's influence, most of our energy resources are channeled to our muscles, preparing us for action. This lowers reserves needed to fight infection and the restorative functions necessary to maintain a healthy body. As a result, we are more susceptible to colds, infections, arthritis, auto-immune diseases, and even cancer—a very bad thing!

By making peace with our anger, practicing forgiveness and increasing self-acceptance and self-love, our health and overall sense of well-being can be improved. This being the case, it is easy to see why we benefit the most when we decide to forgive our enemies quickly and choose to forgive ourself as well . . . becoming our own best friend.

The following is my philosophy of life:

A Healing Gift To Self

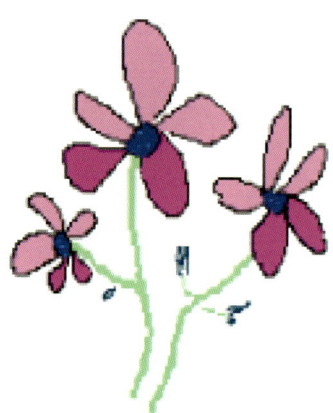

May I always fill myself with sunshine and
empty myself of discontent. I dilute the
pain, the guilt, the sadness of the
past and give myself the peace of mind
that lasts from one moment to the next.
I fill my present with hope at hand, and leave
no room for anxiety's future. For only when I say:
"I am trusting in the fullness of the now, am I giving
myself the blessings of contentment. Forgive? Yes I forgive myself, my family, friends, and foe. I release myself
from bonds of anger, hate, judgment, and self-flagellation
that comes from the past to rob me of my present good-
ness. I allow no robber into my heart or home. For I am
filled with love—the love that I Am brings. I am loved,
and I send love to myself, and all whom I have known.
I release each and every one to his or her own kind
destiny, while I fill myself with joy, health,
success, ever-present sunshine, and oh yes, hope
for bright tomorrows filled with fragrant flowers.

Selected Bibliography

Selected Bibliography

There have been numerous books written that address the topic of forgiveness and/or emotional healing from psychological, child development, sociological, philosophical, and spiritual perspectives. Shedding new light on the plight of this human experience we all share may prove beneficial. Broadening ones base of understanding about the factors that influence behavior will help in our quest to find peace of mind and a healing of the heart and spirit. Most of these reference and resource books listed below can be found in our local libraries. Some might be out of print, but may reside in university libraries or used bookstores. Others may need to be ordered from companies that specialize in locating out of print books. For additional help in finding quality books to assist one on her or his healing journey of self-discovery, go online, visit local bookstores, and speak with a librarian.

Ardrey, Robert. *The Territorial Imperative*. Dell Publishing Co., 1975

Bradshaw, John. *Homecoming: Reclaiming and Championing Your Inner Child*. Bantam Books - 1990

Briggs, Dorothy Corkille. *Your Child's Self-esteem*. Doubleday & Co., 1975

Chopra, Deepok. *Quantum Healing: Exploring The Frontiers of Mind Body Medicine*. New York: Bantam Books, 1990

Frankl, Victor. *Man's Search for Meaning: An Introduction to Logotherapy*. Simon & Schuster, 1963

Glickman, Rosalene. *Optimal Thinking: How to be Your Best Self*. John Wiley & Sons, 2002

Goleman. Daniel. *Emotional Intelligence*. Bantam Books, 1995

Goldstein, Edward Lee. *The Male Thing Explained*. Litas-Hart Publishing, 2005

Jampolsky, Gerald. *Love is Letting Go Of Fear*. Celestial Arts, 1979

McKay, Matthew. *When Anger Hurts*. New Harbinger Publications, 1989

Morris, Desmond. *The Naked Ape*. Dell Publishing Co., 1967

Myss, Caroline. *Why People Don't Heal And How They Can*. Harmony Books, 1997

Siegel, Bernie. *Love, Medicine, & Miracles*. Harper & Roe Publishers, 1988

Smedes, Lewis. *The Art of Forgiving*. Moorings, 1984

Smith, Manuel. *When I Say No I Feel Guilty*. The Dial Press, 1975

About the Author

Author, lecturer, health and holistic educator, physical therapist, intuitive, artist, and devout animal lover; Edward Lee Goldstein defines himself as both healer and mentor. In his approach to wellness, he draws from his diverse academic background consisting of five college degrees, including a Masters in Health Education and a Masters in Art. He brings to the table experiences from worldwide travels and an innate talent for seeing the "big picture." While conducting his consciousness-raising, healing seminars and working with clients in groups or privately, Goldstein embraces humor, the esoteric, and practical information. He believes whether there are physical, emotional, spiritual, and even financial challenges to address, by eclectically integrating the left, analytical brain with the right, intuitive brain, one can heal from the inside out. Using an interactive, cognitive behavioral, anecdotal approach, he imparts the skills and knowledge, which guarantees success.

Edward feels it is important to give back to the community, which has shown him so much support. Dedicated to improving the plight that blighted humanity seems to be facing, he regularly contributes both time and money to worthwhile causes. Among other honors, he was the recipient of the Southern California Motion Picture Council's "Bronze Halo Award.

What sets Edward Lee Goldstein apart from the general population of "experts in the field," is that he does not call himself a "Motivational Speaker"—motivation must come from within. Rather, he views himself as an "Inspiration Generator." In his seminars, such as: "Love, Sex, and the Walking Wounded," Manifesting Your Dreams Through Forgiving Your Nightmares," Edward inspires others to discover the empowering, success-building, health manifesting, joy inspiring motivational skills they already possess. He affirms this current book along with his previous book, *The Male Thing Explained* are catalysts for helping his audience on their healing journeys toward self-acceptance and improved lives.

For inquiries regarding public or corporate speaking engagements, or working privately with Edward Lee Goldstein on relationship and forgiveness issues, physical therapy or other health related areas, visit his website:

Website: **FaithandForgivenessThingExplained.com**
Email: **AskEdward@FaithandForgivenessThingExplained.com**
Phone toll free: **(888) 222-4001**

May the answers you seek bring you the joy you deserve,

Edward Lee Goldstein

Faith's Celestial Song

I always, I always . . . I always was angry, frightened and sad.
Never was happy, always feeling so bad,
Until I found my bliss . . . through forgiveness.

Now I'm feeling a feeling I never felt before.
My heart, my heart is singing a song it never sang before.

Like a rainbow follows rain, a river flows to the sea,
A forgiving heart knows joy, not pain—a new beginning,
Innocence reclaimed.

Like a mother's warm embrace, brings a smile to your face,
When I forgive you, and you forgive me. . . oh how happy we will be.

Like a rainbow follows rain, a river flows to the sea,
A forgiving heart knows joy, not pain—a new beginning,
Innocence, innocence, innocence reclaimed.

Postal Orders:
LITAS-HART Publishing
Edward Lee Goldstein
PO Box 55066
Sherman Oaks, California 91413 USA.

Email: **AskEdward@FaithandForgivenessThingExplained.com**
Web address: **FaithandForgivenessThingExplained.com**
Phone toll free: **(888) 222-4001**

Please send ____copies of *Faith, A Lion's Healing Journey Back To Innocence* @ **$21.95/copy**
plus **sales tax of $2.10/book** plus **shipping costs of $4.00** (within USA) **Total cost: $28.05 for
one book**. (*I will pay shipping on all additional USA purchases.)* **Two books @ $21.95/copy is
$43.90 plus sales tax of** (2 x $2.10) **= $4.20 plus shipping $4.00; Total cost: $52.10 for two
copies.**

Please send ____copies of *The Male Thing Explained* @ **$21.95/copy plus sales tax of $2.10/
book** plus **shipping costs of $4.00** (within USA) **Total cost: $28.05 for one book**. (*Remember,
any purchase of two or more books whether the same or combined titles will save you money.* **The
maximum you'll pay for shipping in the US is $4.00.)**

Make check payable to: LITAS-HART Publishing

Please print clearly when ordering by mail.

Deliver to: **Name** _____

   Address _____

   City _____ **State** _____ **Zip** _____

   Telephone _____

   Email address _____

International Purchases: Please send ____copies of *Faith A Lion's Healing Journey Back To
Innocence* and/or ____copies of The Male Thing Explained @ **$21.95/copy plus shipping costs
of $9.00: Total cost: $30.95 for one book. (For two or more books, add an extra $5.00/book
for shipping and handling.)**

Please send more Free information on:

   __Speaking/Seminars, __Consulting, __Available Art Products/Note Cards

FaithandForgivenessThingExplained.com

Where women and men can go to find the answers they seek

To our loyal readers,

The author, Edward Goldstein, and all of us at LITAS-HART Publishing, thank you for your support. If you found this book to be helpful, please continue to be our partner and recommend it to someone you know. The blessings you give to another, bless you as well. We wish you much bliss on your healing journey.

LITAS-HART Publishing